DAVID & GOLIATH

READ-ALONG STORYBOOK
SING-ALONG SONGS - PC FUN!

Greenbrier International, Inc.
Chesapeake, VA 23320
10732-16000-001-0912
Made in China

David and Goliath
Story adapted by Darcy Weinbeck
Audio CD Reading Performed by David DuChene
Songs Produced and Performed by Deron (D.B.) Harris
Vocal Performances by Melissa Cusick and Deron (D.B.) Harris

ISBN 978-1600720925

First Published 2008

All rights reserved. No part of this publication may be reproduced, stored
in or introduced into a retrieval system, or transmitted, in any
form or by any means (electronic, mechanical, photocopying,
recording or otherwise), for any commercial
purpose without prior written permission.

Long ago, there lived a shepherd boy named David. He lived in the Kingdom of Israel with his family, which included seven older brothers. David's brothers looked down upon him, as he was the youngest and smallest brother. But the Lord didn't see this. He only saw David's big, strong heart. God sent a prophet, Samuel, to anoint David and to declare him the future King of Israel.

TURN PAGE

After David was anointed, he returned to his family's pastures to care for the sheep. He always worked hard to protect the flock. Occasionally, a lion or bear tried to take one of David's sheep from the flock, but David did not allow it. With God at his side, the boy's strength was enough to overcome even lions and bears.

One day, war was declared on the Israelites and their King, Saul, by a group called the Philistines. The Philistines had a plan to take over Israel and to force the Israelites to be their servants. The Israelites had to defend themselves.

David's three eldest brothers joined the fight against the Philistines. They prepared to go to war in support of Israel. David was also courageous and wanted to go, but he knew that his place was at home, protecting the sheep.

After forty days of war, David's father asked David to go to the battle area and find his brothers. His father packed a load of food to replenish his military sons' supply. David agreed to go on the journey.

TURN PAGE

David found a keeper to watch his sheep, and he left right away to find the three brothers, just as his father had requested. It was a long, hot walk. But he knew that seeing his brothers again would be worth it.

When David found the Israelite battle camp, he was surprised to see the number of tents and soldiers. He became aware of the great size of the battle and wished that he could help in some way. **TURN PAGE**

David realized that the one way that he could help was by fulfilling his dad's wish. He needed to find his brothers and give them the load of food. Thankfully, another soldier was able to direct David to his brothers' tent.

The three eldest brothers greeted David. David gave them the food their father sent. The sight of the food seemed to overwhelm the brothers. They had been hungry for a very long time.

TURN PAGE

Sound of chaos outside the tent interrupted the brotherly reunion. All four brothers rushed out of the tent to see what was happening. They were surprised to find a looming shadow of a giant standing in opposition.

The three oldest brothers were terrified because they knew who was creating the shadow. It was the giant Philistine, Goliath. He was over nine feet tall. The ground shook as Goliath stepped forward and shouted, "Who among you dares to fight me? We will only stop this war when I am defeated." David watched as many of the Israelite soldiers fled.

But David stood up straight, his three brothers at his side. "Who is going to stop that beast?" David asked his brothers as he watched the giant continue to prod the crowd. "No one," they replied. For the brothers knew that no normal-sized man could conquer him.

What the three oldest brothers did not know was that there was someone present who was not of normal size. His body was actually quite small, but his heart was gigantic. He had the courage of no other. The three brothers looked at David watching Goliath and they suddenly became worried.

TURN PAGE

David started to step toward Goliath, but his brothers stopped him. "He will kill you," one brother pleaded. David replied, "But I have God on my side and He gives me the courage and the wisdom to defeat this beast." He knew that he was the only one that could defeat Goliath.

Soldiers overheard David talking with his brothers and went and told the King of Israel the news. King Saul could not believe what he was hearing. Could it be that there was a soul brave enough to fight Goliath? If someone could actually beat Goliath, the Israelites would be free of this war.

TURN PAGE

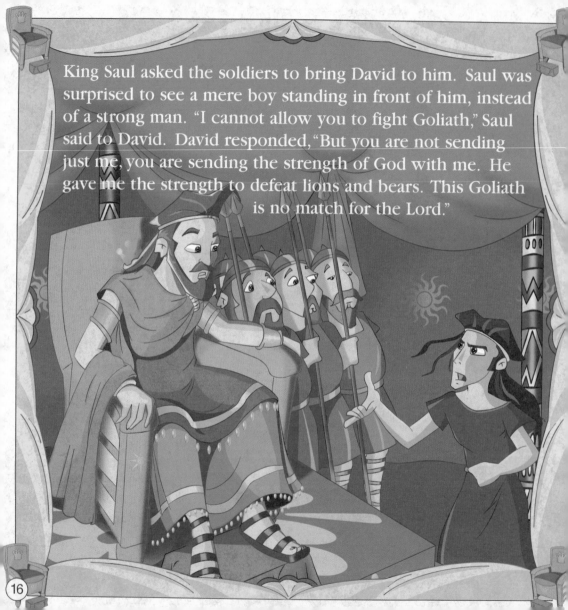

King Saul asked the soldiers to bring David to him. Saul was surprised to see a mere boy standing in front of him, instead of a strong man. "I cannot allow you to fight Goliath," Saul said to David. David responded, "But you are not sending just me, you are sending the strength of God with me. He gave me the strength to defeat lions and bears. This Goliath is no match for the Lord."

King Saul listened to David's words and believed that it might be possible for the young boy to conquer the giant. King Saul offered David armor and a sword to defeat Goliath. "I will pray for God to be with you."

TURN PAGE

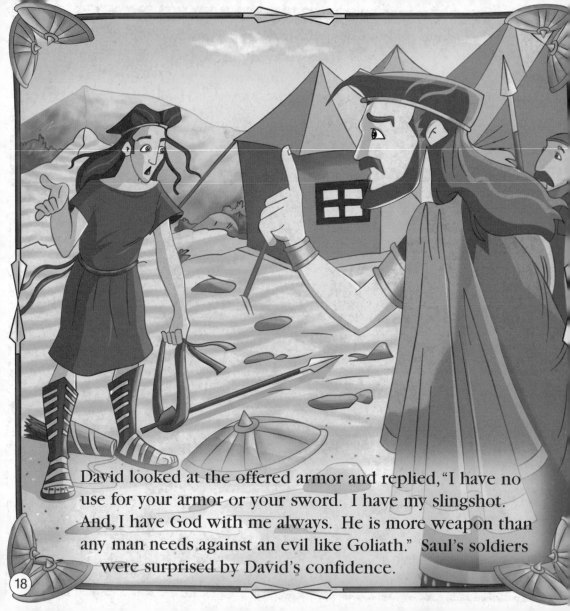

David looked at the offered armor and replied, "I have no use for your armor or your sword. I have my slingshot. And, I have God with me always. He is more weapon than any man needs against an evil like Goliath." Saul's soldiers were surprised by David's confidence.

David left Saul and headed toward the Philistine camp, slingshot in hand. All he needed was a few rocks for his weapon. He stopped at a small stream and found some for his pouch. He grabbed five smooth stones, but he knew that with God's strength and wisdom, he would only need one stone to take down Goliath.

TURN PAGE

David made it to the edge of the Philistine camp and called out for Goliath. Goliath and the Philistine soldiers looked on in amusement. David yelled, "Goliath, you have challenged the Israelites with a battle of swords and spears. I have come to you with even more strength. I come to you in the name of the Lord, the God of the armies of Israel."

Goliath became angry at such words. He looked at David's shepherd's staff, pouch of rocks, and slingshot and yelled, "You believe that I am some dog that you can scare me away with mere sticks and stones, child?" David responded with a confident stare and said, "You are forgetting my weapon of greatness, the Lord, my God."

TURN PAGE

With that, Goliath's anger grew even more intense. Goliath drew his sword. David prepared his slingshot with a single stone. Soldiers from both camps watched as David and Goliath faced off.

Goliath swung his sword at David, but missed. David, however, slung his stone with perfect aim.

The stone shot through the air and struck Goliath in the forehead, sending the giant Philistine to his knees and to his death. The Israelite army cheered for David who had saved them from the evil Goliath and from the Philistines.

David returned to his home. And eventually he became King of Israel, just as the prophet Samuel had declared. David's life was a journey that led him from tending his sheep, to being anointed, meeting King Saul, conquering Goliath, and becoming King, all the while with God at his side.

SAMSON AND DELILAH
Read-Along Storybook
Sing-Along Songs
PC Fun!
Noah's Ark
Read-Along Storybook • Sing-Along Songs • PC Fun!
Enjoy All 4 Stories!
JONAH AND THE WHALE
SING-ALONG SONGS • PC FUN!
DAVID AND GOLIATH